Handbook of Lions

Editor

Loree Vallejo

Scribbles

Year of Publication 2018

ISBN : 9789352979790

Book Published by

Scribbles

(An Imprint of Alpha Editions)

email - alphaedis@gmail.com

Produced by: PediaPress GmbH
Limburg an der Lahn
Germany
http://pediapress.com/

Contents

Lion

<indicator name="pp-default"> 🔒 </indicator>

<indicator name="featured-star"> ⭐ </indicator>

Lion
Temporal range: Pleistocene–Present Pre꞊Є꞊ OSD C P T J K Pg꞊N

Male lion in Okonjima, Namibia

Female (lioness) in Okonjima
Conservation status
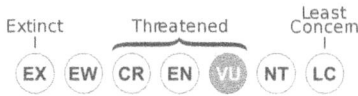 Vulnerable (IUCN 3.1)
Scientific classification 🖉

Kingdom:	Animalia

Phylum:	Chordata
Class:	Mammalia
Order:	Carnivora
Suborder:	Feliformia
Family:	Felidae
Subfamily:	Pantherinae
Genus:	*Panthera*
Species:	*P. leo*
Binomial name	
Panthera leo (Linnaeus, 1758)	
Subspecies	
P. l. leo *P. l. melanochaita* † *P. l. sinhaleyus*	

Historical and present distribution of *Panthera leo* in Africa, Asia and Europe

The **lion** (*Panthera leo*) is a species in the family Felidae; it is a muscular, deep-chested cat with a short, rounded head, a reduced neck and round ears, and a hairy tuft at the end of its tail. The lion is sexually dimorphic; males are larger than females with a typical weight range of 150 to 250 kg (330 to 550 lb) for the former and 120 to 182 kg (265 to 400 lb) for the latter. Male lions have a prominent mane, which is the most recognisable feature of the species. A lion pride consists of a few adult males, related females and cubs. Groups of female lions typically hunt together, preying mostly on large ungulates. The species is an apex and keystone predator, although they scavenge when opportunities occur. Some lions have been known to hunt humans, although the species typically does not.

Typically, the lion inhabits grasslands and savannas but is absent in dense forests. It is usually more diurnal than other big cats, but when persecuted it adapts to being active at night and at twilight. In the Pleistocene, the lion ranged throughout Eurasia, Africa and the Americas from the Yukon to Peru but today it has been reduced to fragmented populations in Sub-Saharan Africa and one critically endangered population in western India. It has been listed as Vulnerable on the IUCN Red List since 1996 because populations in African countries have declined by about 43% since the early 1990s. Lion populations are untenable outside designated protected areas. Although the cause of the decline is not fully understood, habitat loss and conflicts with humans are the greatest causes for concern.

One of the most widely recognised animal symbols in human culture, the lion has been extensively depicted in sculptures and paintings, on national flags, and in contemporary films and literature. Lions have been kept in menageries since the time of the Roman Empire and have been a key species sought for exhibition in zoological gardens across the world since the late 18th century. Cultural depictions of lions were prominent in the Upper Paleolithic period; carvings and paintings from the Lascaux and Chauvet Caves in France have been dated to 17,000 years ago, and depictions have occurred in virtually all ancient and medieval cultures that coincided with the lion's former and current ranges.

Etymology

The lion's name, which is similar in many Romance languages, is derived from *Latin: leo* and Ancient Greek: λέων (*leon*). The word *lavi* (Hebrew: לָבִיא) may also be related.

Taxonomy and phylogeny

In 1758, Carl Linnaeus described the lion in his work *Systema Naturae* and gave it the scientific name *Felis leo*. Between the mid-18th and mid-20th centuries, 26 lion specimens were described and proposed as subspecies, of which 11 were recognised as valid in 2005. They were distinguished on the basis of appearance, size and colour of mane. Because these characteristics show much variation between individuals, most of these forms were probably not true subspecies, especially because they were often based upon museum material with "striking, but abnormal" morphological characteristics.

Based on the morphology of 58 lion skulls in three European museums, the subspecies *krugeri*, *nubica*, *persica* and *senegalensis* were assessed distinct but

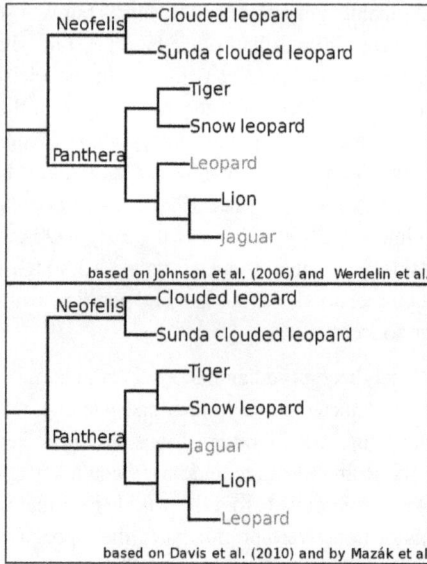

Figure 1: *Two cladograms proposed for Panthera. The upper cladogram is based on the 2006 and 2009 studies, while the lower one is based on the 2010 and 2011 studies.*

bleyenberghi overlapped with *senegalensis* and *krugeri*. The Asiatic lion *persica* was the most distinctive and the Cape lion had characteristics allying it more with *persica* than the other sub-Saharan lions.

The lion's closest relatives are the other species of the genus *Panthera*; the tiger, snow leopard, jaguar, and leopard. Results of phylogenetic studies published in 2006 and 2009 indicate that the jaguar and the lion belong to one sister group that diverged about 2.06 million years ago. Results of later studies published in 2010 and 2011 indicate that the leopard and the lion belong to the same sister group, which diverged between 1.95 and 3.10 million years ago. Hybridisation between lion and snow leopard populations, however, may have continued until about 2.1 million years ago.

Evolution and genetic diversity

The lion evolved between 1 million and 800,000 years ago in Africa, from where it spread throughout the Holarctic region. The earliest fossil record in Europe was found near Pakefield in the United Kingdom and is about 680,000 years old. From this lion, the late Pleistocene Eurasian cave lion probably derived about 300,000 years ago. Fossil remains found in the Cromer Forest Bed

Figure 2: *Cave lion (Panthera spelaea) with a reindeer. Painting by Heinrich Harder.*

suggest it was of a gigantic size and represented a lineage that was genetically isolated and highly distinct from lions in Africa and Asia. It was distributed throughout Europe, across Siberia and into western Alaska via the Beringian landmass. The gradual formation of dense forest likely caused the decline of its geographic range near the end of the Late Pleistocene. Lion bones are frequently encountered in cave deposits from Eemian times, suggesting the cave lion survived in the Balkans and Asia Minor. There was probably a continuous population extending into India. Fossil lion remains were found in Pleistocene deposits in West Bengal. It became extinct about 10,000 years ago at the end of the last glacial period without mitochondrial descendants on other continents.

A fossil carnassial found in the Batadomba Cave indicates that *Panthera leo sinhaleyus* inhabited Sri Lanka during the late Pleistocene, and is thought to have become extinct around 39,000 years ago. This subspecies was described by Deraniyagala in 1939. It is distinct from the contemporary lion.

During the last glacial maximum until about 20,000 years ago, the lion was likely distributed throughout most of Southern and Central Africa, and expanded its range northwards during the early Holocene about 10,000 to 4,000 years ago. Early phylogenetic research was focused on lions from eastern and southern parts of Africa, and already showed they can possibly be divided in two main clades; one to the west and the other to the east of the East African Rift. Lions in eastern Kenya are genetically much closer to lions in Southern Africa than to lions in Aberdare National Park in western Kenya.

In a subsequent study, tissue and bone samples of 32 lion specimens in museums were used. Results indicated lions form three phylogeographic groups: one each in Asia and North Africa, in Central Africa and in Southern Africa. Samples of 53 lions, both wild and captive, from 15 countries were used for phylogenetic analysis. Results showed little genetic diversity among lion samples from Asia and West and Central Africa, whereas samples from East and Southern Africa revealed numerous mutations indicating this group has a longer evolutionary history.

Results of subsequent phylogeographic research indicate that the species diverged into the northern and southern lineages about 245,000 years ago. Extinction of lions in southern Europe and the Middle East interrupted gene flow between lions in Asia and Africa.

Approximately 77% of the captive lions registered in the International Species Information System in 2006 were of unknown origin; these animals might have carried genes that are extinct in the wild and may therefore be important to the maintenance of the overall genetic variability of the lion. Lions imported to Europe before the middle of the 19th century were possibly foremost Barbary lions from North Africa, or Cape lions from Southern Africa.

Subspecies

In the 19th and 20th centuries, several lion type specimen were described and proposed as subspecies: At least a dozen recent (Holocene) subspecies were recognised before 2017, including nine for East Africa:

Between 2008 and 2016, IUCN Red List assessors for lions used only two subspecific names; *P. l. leo* for African lion populations and *P. l. persica* for the Asiatic lion population. In 2017, the Cat Classification Task Force of the Cat Specialist Group revised classification of subspecies based on phylogeographic research, while acknowledging that morphological diagnoses were not known:

- *P. l. leo* (Linnaeus, 1758) is the nominate lion subspecies and includes the regionally extinct Barbary lion, as well as the Asiatic, West African and Central African lion populations. Former synonyms include *P. l. persica* (Meyer, 1826), *P. l. senegalensis* (Meyer, 1826), *P. l. kamptzi* (Matschie, 1900), and *P. l. azandica* (Allen, 1924).
- *P. l. melanochaita* (Smith, 1842) includes the extinct Cape lion, the East and Southern African lion populations. Former synonyms include *P. l. massaica* (Neumann, 1900), *P. l. sabakiensis* (Lönnberg, 1910), *P. l. bleyenberghi* (Lönnberg, 1914), *P. l. roosevelti* (Heller, 1914), *P. l. nyanzae* (Heller, 1914), *P. l. hollisteri* (Allen, 1924), *P. l. krugeri* (Roberts, 1929), *P. l. vernayi* (Roberts, 1948) and *P. l. webbiensis* (Zukowsky, 1964).

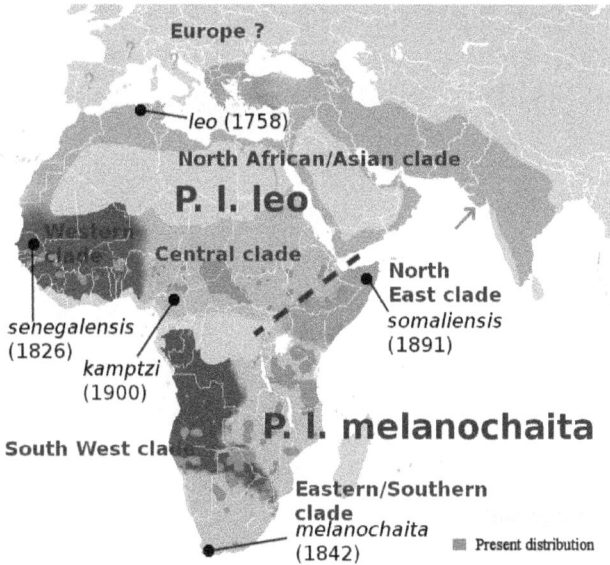

Figure 3: *Range map including proposed clades and the two subspecies (P. l. leo and P. l. melanochaita) according to genetic research*

There is phylogenetic evidence that Ethiopia was a contact zone between the two subspecies. Wild lion samples from Gambela and Bale Mountains National Parks and eastern Ethiopia exhibited haplotypes that grouped with the Central African lion clade, whereas lion samples from southwestern Ethiopia grouped with samples from Somalia and Kenya.

Extinct species and subspecies

Other lion subspecies or sister species to the modern lion existed in prehistoric times:

- *P. l. fossilis or Panthera fossilis* bone fragments excavated in Germany, United Kingdom, Italy and Czech Republic have been estimated to be between 680,000 and 600,000 years old. The animal was larger than the modern lion.
- *Panthera spelaea* or Eurasian cave lion bone fragments were excavated in Europe, North Asia, Canada and Alaska. It probably became extinct between 14,900 and 11,900 years ago. The oldest known bone fragments are estimated to be between 109,000 and 57,000 years old. It is depicted in Paleolithic cave paintings, ivory carvings, and clay busts, which show it as having protruding ears, tufted tails and faint, tiger-like stripes. A few specimens are depicted with ruffs around their necks.

Figure 4: *An American Lion skull at the National Museum of Natural History*

- *P. l. atrox* or *P. atrox*, known as the American lion or American cave lion, existed in the Americas from Canada to Peru in the Pleistocene Epoch until about 10,000 years ago. This form is a sister clade of *P. spelaea* that likely arose when an early *P. spelaea* population became isolated south of the North American continental ice sheet about 340,000 years ago. It is among the largest purported lion subspecies to have existed; its body length is estimated to have been 1.6–2.5 m (5.2–8.2 ft).

Dubious subspecies

- *P. l. youngi* or *Panthera youngi* flourished 350,000 years ago. Its relationship to the extant lion subspecies is obscure; it probably represents a distinct species.
- *P. l. mesopotamica* was described on the basis of a relief from the Neo-Assyrian Period made between 1000 BC and 600 BC in ancient Mesopotamia.
- *P. l. europaea* was proposed for subfossil remains of lions excavated in Southern Europe that date to between the Late Neolithic and the Early Iron Age.
- *P. l. maculatus*, known as the Marozi or spotted lion, is sometimes thought to be a distinct subspecies but may be an adult lion that has retained its juvenile spotted pattern. If it was a subspecies rather than a

Figure 5: *A cylinder seal from Elam, Iran, featuring an adaptation of the Babylonian lion hunt theme, 800–600 BC, now at the Walters Art Museum*

small number of aberrantly coloured individuals, it has been extinct since 1931. It also may have been a natural leopard-lion hybrid commonly known as a leopon, although this is a less-likely identification.

Hybrids

Lions have been bred with tigers, most often the Siberian and Bengal tigers, to create hybrids called "ligers" and "tiglons" or "tigons". They also have been crossed with leopards to produce "leopons". Such hybrid breeding is now discouraged because of the emphasis on conserving species and subspecies. Hybrids are still bred in private menageries and in zoos in China.(in Chamorro)

The liger is a cross between a male lion and a tigress. Because the growth-inhibiting gene from the tiger mother is absent, the growth-promoting gene passed on by the lion father is unimpeded by a regulating gene and the resulting liger grows far larger than either parent. The liger inherits the physical and behavioural qualities of both parent species; for example, its coat has both spots and stripes on a sandy background. Male ligers are sterile but females often are fertile. Males have about a 50% chance of having a mane, which will be around 50% the size of a pure-bred lion mane. Ligers are much bigger than normal lions and tigers; they are typically 3.65 m (12.0 ft) in length, and can weigh up to 500 kg (1,100 lb).

The less-common tiglon or tigon is a cross between a lioness and a male tiger. In contrast to ligers, tigons are often relatively small in comparison with their parents because of reciprocal gene effects.

Description

The lion is a muscular, deep-chested cat with a short, rounded head, a reduced neck and round ears. Its fur varies in colour from light buff to silvery grey, yellowish red and dark brown. The colours of the underparts are generally lighter. When they are born, have dark spots on their bodies; these spots fade as the cubs reach adulthood, although faint spots often may still be seen on the legs and underparts. The lion is the only member of the cat family that displays obvious sexual dimorphism. Males are more robust than females; they have broader heads and a prominent mane that grows downwards and backwards to cover most of the head, neck, shoulders, and chest. The mane is typically brownish and tinged with yellow, rust and black hairs. The tail ends in a dark, hairy tuft that in some lions conceals an approximately 5 mm (0.20 in)-long, hard "spine" or "spur" that is formed from the final, fused sections of tail bone. The functions of the spur are unknown. The tuft is absent at birth and develops at around 5 $^1/_2$ months of age and is readily identifiable by the age of seven months.[1]

Of the living, non-hybrid felids, the lion is rivalled only by the tiger in length, weight and height at the shoulder. Its skull is very similar to that of the tiger, although the frontal region is usually more depressed and flattened, and has a slightly shorter postorbital region and broader nasal openings than those of the tiger. Due to the amount of skull variation in the two species, usually only the structure of the lower jaw can be used as a reliable indicator of species. The size and weight of adult lions varies across global range and habitats.

Average	Female lions	Male lions
Head-and-body length	140–175 cm (4 ft 7 in–5 ft 9 in)	170–298 cm (5 ft 7 in–9 ft 9 in)
Tail length	70–100 cm (2 ft 4 in–3 ft 3 in)	90–105 cm (2 ft 11 in–3 ft 5 in)
Weight	120–182 kg (265–401 lb), 124.2–139.8 kg (274–308 lb) in Southern Africa, 119.5 kg (263 lb) in East Africa, 110–120 kg (240–260 lb) in India	150–250 kg (330–550 lb), 187.5–193.3 kg (413–426 lb) in Southern Africa, 174.9 kg (386 lb) in East Africa, 160–190 kg (350–420 lb) in India

Accounts of a few individuals that were larger than average exist from Africa and India. For the Pleistocene American lion, a study in 2012 estimated a weight range of 235–523 kg (518–1,153 pounds) for males and 175–365 kg (386–805 pounds) for females.

Mane

<templatestyles src="Multiple_image/styles.css" />

A captive Asiatic male with a thick mane that is mostly dark

A maneless lion in Tsavo East National Park, Kenya

The lion's mane is the most recognisable feature of the species. It starts growing when lions are about a year old. Mane colour varies and darkens with age; research shows its colour and size are influenced by environmental factors such as average ambient temperature. Mane length apparently signals fighting success in male–male relationships; darker-maned individuals may have longer reproductive lives and higher offspring survival, although they suffer in the hottest months of the year. The presence, absence, colour and size of the mane are associated with genetic precondition, sexual maturity, climate and testosterone production; the rule of thumb is that a darker, fuller mane indicates a healthier animal. In Serengeti National Park, female lions favour males with dense, dark manes as mates. The main purpose of the mane is thought be the protection of the neck and throat in territorial fights with rivals. Cool ambient temperature in European and North American zoos may result in a heavier mane. Asiatic lions usually have sparser manes than average African lions.

Almost all West African males In the area of Pendjari National Park are either maneless or have very insubstantial manes. Maneless male African lions have also been reported in Senegal, in Sudan's Dinder National Park and in Tsavo East National Park, Kenya. The original male white lion from Timbavati was also maneless. The hormone testosterone has been linked to mane growth; castrated lions often have little to no mane because the removal of the gonads

Figure 6: *White lions owe their colouring to a recessive allele*

inhibits testosterone production. Increased testosterone may be the cause of maned lionesses reported in northern Botswana.

Cave paintings of extinct European cave lions almost exclusively show hunting animals with no manes; some suggest this is evidence the males of this species were maneless. Because the hunting usually involved groups of lionesses, however, this presumption remains unproven. In the Chauvet Cave is a sketchy drawing of two maneless lions that appearing to be walking side-by-side. One lion is mostly obscured by the other; the obscuring lion is larger than the obscured one and is depicted with a scrotum.

Colour variation

The white lion is a rare morph with a genetic condition called leucism that is caused by a double recessive allele. It is not albino; it has normal pigmentation in the eyes and skin. White lions have occasionally been encountered in and around Kruger National Park and the adjacent Timbavati Private Game Reserve in eastern South Africa. They were removed from the wild in the 1970s, thus decreasing the white lion gene pool. Nevertheless, 17 births have been recorded in five prides between 2007 and 2015. White lions are selected for breeding in captivity. They have reportedly been bred in camps in South Africa for use as trophies to be killed during canned hunts.

Figure 7: *Adult male lion stretching in Etosha National Park, Namibia*

A melanistic Asiatic lion from Khuzestan, Iran, which was dark brown with nearly black patches, was described by Austen Henry Layard.

Behaviour and ecology

Lions spend much of their time resting; they are inactive for about 20 hours per day.[2] Although lions can be active at any time, their activity generally peaks after dusk with a period of socialising, grooming and defecating. Intermittent bursts of activity continue until dawn, when hunting most often takes place. They spend an average of two hours a day walking and 50 minutes eating.[3]

Group organisation

<templatestyles src="Multiple_image/styles.css" />

A pride of lion headed by one male at Masai Mara, Kenya

A lioness (left) and two males at Masai Mara

Tree-climbing lions of Ishasha, Queen Elizabeth National Park, Uganda

The lion is the most social of all wild cat species, living in groups of related individuals with their offspring. Such a group is called a "pride". Groups of male lions are called "coalitions".[4] Females form the stable social unit in a pride and do not tolerate outside females.[5] Membership only changes with the births and deaths of lionesses,[6] although some females leave and become nomadic.[7] The average pride consists of around 15 lions, including several adult females and up to four males and their cubs of both sexes. Large prides, consisting of up to 30 individuals, have been observed.[8] The sole exception to this pattern is the Tsavo lion pride that always has just one adult male. Male cubs are excluded from their maternal pride when they reach maturity at around two or three years of age.

Some lions are "nomads" that range widely and move around sporadically, either in pairs or alone. Pairs are more frequent among related males who have been excluded from their birth pride. A lion may switch lifestyles; nomads can become residents and vice versa. Interactions between prides and nomads tend to be hostile, although pride females in estrous allow nomadic males to approach them.[9] Males spend years in a nomadic phase before gaining residence in a pride. A study undertaken in the Serengeti National Park revealed that nomadic coalitions gain residency at between 3.5 and 7.3 years of age. In Kruger National Park, dispersing male lions move more than 25 km away from their natal pride in search of their own territory. Females lions stay closer to their natal pride. Therefore, female lions in an area are more closely related to each other than male lions in the same area.

The area occupied by a pride is called a "pride area" whereas that occupied by a nomad is a "range". Males associated with a pride tend to stay on the fringes, patrolling their territory. The reasons for the development of sociality in lionesses – the most pronounced in any cat species – are the subject of much debate. Increased hunting success appears to be an obvious reason, but this is uncertain upon examination; coordinated hunting allows for more successful predation but also ensures non-hunting members reduce *per capita* calorific intake. Some females, however, take a role raising cubs that may be left alone for extended periods. Members of the pride tend to regularly play the same role in hunts and hone their skills. The health of the hunters is the primary need for the survival of the pride; hunters are the first to consume the prey at the site it is taken. Other benefits include possible kin selection – it is preferable to share food with a related lion than with a stranger – protection of the young, maintenance of territory and individual insurance against injury and hunger.

Both males and females defend the pride against intruders but the male lion is better-suited for this purpose due to its stockier, more powerful build.[10] Some individuals consistently lead the defence against intruders, while others lag behind. Lions tend to assume specific roles in the pride; slower-moving individuals may provide other valuable services to the group. Alternatively, there may be rewards associated with being a leader that fends off intruders; the rank of lionesses in the pride is reflected in these responses. The male or males associated with the pride must defend their relationship with the pride from outside males who may attempt to usurp them.

Asiatic lion prides differ from African prides in group composition. Male Asiatic lions are solitary or associate with up to three males, forming a loose pride. Pairs of males rest and feed together, and display marking behaviour at the same sites. Females associate with up to 12 other females, forming a stronger pride together with their cubs. They share large carcasses with each other but seldom share food with males. Female and male lions associate only when mating. Coalitions of males hold territory for a longer time than single lions. Males in coalitions of three or four individuals exhibit a pronounced hierarchy, in which one male dominates the others. Dominant males mate more frequently than their coalition partners; during a study carried out between December 2012 and December 2016, three females were observed switching mating partners in favour of the dominant male.

Hunting and diet

<templatestyles src="Multiple_image/styles.css" />

A lion's teeth are typical of a carnivore

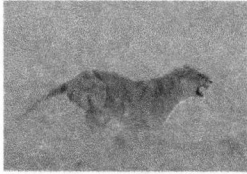

Lioness in a burst of speed while hunting in the Serengeti

Four lionesses catching a cape buffalo in the Serengeti

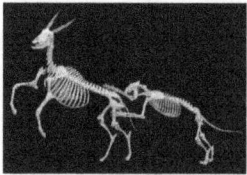

A skeletal mount of an African lion attacking a common eland on display at The Museum of Osteology, Oklahoma City

The lion is a generalist hypercarnivore and usually hunts in groups. Its prey consists mainly of mammals – particularly ungulates – with a preference for blue wildebeest, plains zebra, African buffalo, gemsbok and giraffe. Because of its wide prey spectrum, the lion is considered to be an apex and keystone predator. Lions prefer prey weighing 190–550 kg (420–1,210 lb). They usually avoid fully grown adult elephants, rhinoceroses and hippopotamus, as well as small prey like dik-dik, hyrax, hare and vervet monkey.[11] Lions do hunt common warthog depending on availability, although the species is below the preferred weight range. Lions also attack domestic livestock that, in India, contribute significantly to their diet. Unusual prey items include porcupines and small reptiles. Lions kill other predators such as leopard, cheetah and spotted hyena but seldom consume them.[12]

In many areas, a small number of species comprise a majority of the lion's diet. In Serengeti National Park, wildebeest, zebra and Thompson's gazelle form the majority of lion prey.[13] In Kruger National Park, giraffe, zebra and buffalo are the most commonly hunted. In Manyara Park, buffalo was estimated to constitute about 62% of the lion's meat consumption. In Gir Forest National Park in India, sambar deer and chital are the most commonly recorded wild prey. In the Okavango Delta, potential prey migrate seasonally. Up to eight species comprise three quarters of a lion's diet. The size and aquatic nature of hippopotamus means it is normally unavailable as prey but lions in Virunga National Park occasionally hunt hippopotamus calves and in Gorongosa National Park they also take adult specimens.[14] In the Savuti marsh in Botswana's Chobe National Park, lions have been recorded hunting juvenile and sub-adult African bush elephants during the dry season, when ungulates migrate away from the area. In October 2005, a pride of up to 30 lions killed and consumed eight African bush elephants that were between four and eleven years old. The prey-to-predator weight ratio of 10–15:1 between elephants and lions is the highest ratio known among terrestrial mammals.

Young lions first display stalking behaviour at around three months of age, although they do not participate in hunting until they are almost a year old and begin to hunt effectively when nearing the age of two.[15] Single lions are capable of bringing down prey twice their size, such as zebra and wildebeest, while hunting larger prey like giraffes and buffalo alone is too risky. Cooperatively hunting lions are usually successful.[16] In prides, lionesses do most of the hunting. In typical hunts, each lioness has a favoured position in the group, either stalking prey on the "wing" then attacking or moving a smaller distance in the centre of the group and capturing prey fleeing from other lionesses. Males attached to prides do not usually participate in group hunting. Some evidence suggests, however, that males are just as successful as females; they are typically solo hunters who ambush prey in small bushland. Lions are not particularly known for their stamina – for instance, a lioness' heart comprises only 0.57% of her body weight and a male's is about 0.45% of his body weight, whereas a hyena's heart comprises almost 1% of its body weight.[17] Thus, lions only run quickly in short bursts[18] and need to be close to their prey before starting the attack. They take advantage of factors that reduce visibility; many kills take place near some form of cover or at night.[19] Because lions are ambush hunters, human farmers have recently found that lions are easily discouraged if they think their prey has seen them. To protect their cattle from such attacks with that knowledge in mind, farmers have found it effective to paint eyes on the hindquarters of each cow, which is usually enough to make hunting lions think they have been seen and select easier prey.

The lion's attack is short and powerful; they attempt to catch prey with a fast rush and final leap, and usually kill prey by strangulation, which can cause cerebral ischemia or asphyxia and results in hypoxaemia or hypoxia. They also kill prey by enclosing its mouth and nostrils in their jaws, which also results in asphyxia. Lions typically consume prey at the location of the hunt but sometimes drag large prey into cover. They tend to squabble over kills, particularly the males. Cubs suffer most when food is scarce but otherwise all pride members eat their fill, including old and crippled lions, which can live on leftovers. Large kills are shared more widely among pride members.[20] An adult lioness requires an average of about 5 kg (11 lb) of meat per day while males require about 7 kg (15 lb).[21] Lions gorge themselves and eat up to 30 kg (66 lb) in one session; if it is unable to consume all of the kill, it rests for a few hours before continuing to eat. On hot days, the pride retreats to shade with one or two males standing guard.[22] Lions defend their kills from scavengers such as vultures and hyenas.

Lions scavenge on carrion when the opportunity arises; they scavenge animals dead from natural causes such as disease or those that were killed by other predators. Scavenging lions keep a constant lookout for circling vultures, which indicate the death or distress of an animal.[23] Most carrion on which both hyenas and lions feed upon are killed by hyenas rather than lions. Carrion is thought to provide a large part of lion diet.

Predator competition

Lions and spotted hyenas occupy a similar ecological niche and where they coexist they compete for prey and carrion; a review of data across several studies indicates a dietary overlap of 58.6%. Lions typically ignore spotted hyenas unless the lions are on a kill or are being harassed by the hyenas, while the latter tend to visibly react to the presence of lions, with or without the presence of food. Lions seize the kills of spotted hyenas; in the Ngorongoro crater it is common for lions to subsist largely on kills stolen from hyenas, causing the hyenas to increase their kill rate. In Botswana's Chobe National Park, the situation is reversed; hyenas frequently challenge lions and steal their kills, obtaining food from 63% of all lion kills. When confronted on a kill by lions, spotted hyenas may either leave or wait patiently at a distance of 30–100 m (100–330 ft) until the lions have finished.[24] Hyenas are bold enough to feed alongside lions and to force the lions off a kill. The two species attack

Figure 8: *Lion attacked by spotted hyenas in Sabi Sand Game Reserve, South Africa*

one another even when there is no food involved for no apparent reason.[25] Lion predation can account for up to 71% of hyena deaths in Etosha National Park. Spotted hyenas have adapted by frequently mobbing lions that enter their territories. When the lion population in Kenya's Masai Mara National Reserve declined, the spotted hyena population increased rapidly. Experiments on captive spotted hyenas show that specimens without prior experience with lions act indifferently to the sight of them, but will react fearfully to lion scent. The size of male lions allows them to occasionally confront hyenas in otherwise evenly matched brawls and decide the balance in favour of the lions.

Lions tend to dominate smaller felids such as cheetahs and leopards where they coexist; lions steal the kills and kill the cubs – and even adults when given the chance.[26] The cheetah in particular has a 50% chance of losing its kills to lions or other predators. Lions are major killers of cheetah cubs, in one study accounting for up to 78.2% of predator-killed juveniles. Cheetahs avoid their competitors by using different temporal (time) and spatial (habitat) niches. Leopards are able to take refuge in trees; lionesses, however, will occasionally be successful in climbing to retrieve leopard kills.[27] Lions similarly dominate African wild dogs, taking their kills and preying on young and rarely adult dogs. Population densities of wild dogs are low in areas where lions are more abundant. However, there are a few reported cases of old and wounded lions falling prey to wild dogs.[28] Lions may also conflict with Nile crocodiles; depending on the sizes of the crocodile and the lion, either can lose kills or carrion to the other. Lions have been known to kill crocodiles venturing onto land, while the reverse is true for lions entering waterways, evidenced by the occasional lion claw found in crocodile stomachs.

Figure 9: *Lioness stealing a kill from a leopard in Kruger National Park, South Africa*

Reproduction and life cycle

<templatestyles src="Multiple_image/styles.css" />

Lions mating at Masai Mara

A lion cub in Masai Mara

Most lionesses reproduce by the time they are four years of age.[29] Lions do not mate at a specific time of year and the females are polyestrous.[30] Like those of other cats, the male lion's penis has spines that point backward. During withdrawal of the penis, the spines rake the walls of the female's vagina, which may cause ovulation.[31] A lioness may mate with more than one male when she is in heat.[32]

Generation length of the lion is about seven years. The average gestation period is around 110 days; the female gives birth to a litter of between one and four cubs in a secluded den, which may be a thicket, a reed-bed, a cave, or some other sheltered area, usually away from the pride. She will often hunt alone while the cubs are still helpless, staying relatively close to the den.[33] Lion cubs are born blind – their eyes open around seven days after birth. They weigh 1.2–2.1 kg (2.6–4.6 lb) at birth and are almost helpless, beginning to crawl a day or two after birth and walking around three weeks of age.[34] To avoid a buildup of scent attracting the attention of predators, the lioness moves her cubs to a new den site several times a month, carrying them one-by-one by the nape of the neck.

Usually, the mother does not integrate herself and her cubs back into the pride until the cubs are six to eight weeks old. Sometimes this introduction to pride life occurs earlier, particularly if other lionesses have given birth at about the same time. Pride lionesses often synchronise their reproductive cycles and communal rearing and suckling of the young, which suckle indiscriminately from any or all of the nursing females in the pride. The synchronization of births is advantageous because the cubs grow to being roughly the same size and have an equal chance of survival, and sucklings are not dominated by older cubs.[35]

When first introduced to the rest of the pride, lion cubs lack confidence when confronted with adults other than their mother. They soon begin to immerse themselves in the pride life, however, playing among themselves or attempting to initiate play with the adults. Lionesses with cubs of their own are more likely to be tolerant of another lioness's cubs than lionesses without cubs. Male tolerance of the cubs varies – sometimes a male will patiently let the cubs play with his tail or his mane, whereas another may snarl and bat the cubs away.[36]

Weaning occurs after six or seven months. Male lions reach maturity at about three years of age and at four to five years are capable of challenging and displacing adult males associated with another pride. They begin to age and weaken at between 10 and 15 years of age at the latest. When one or more new males oust the previous males associated with a pride, the victors often kill any existing young cubs, perhaps because females do not become fertile and receptive until their cubs mature or die. Females often fiercely defend their cubs from a usurping male but are rarely successful unless a group of three or

Figure 10: *Video of a lioness and her cubs in*
Phinda Private Game Reserve, South Africa

four mothers within a pride join forces against the male. Cubs also die from starvation and abandonment, and predation by leopards, hyenas and wild dogs. Up to 80% of lion cubs will die before the age of two.

Both male and female lions may be ousted from prides to become nomads, although most females usually remain with their birth pride. When a pride becomes too large, however, the youngest generation of female cubs may be forced to leave to find their own territory. When a new male lion takes over a pride, adolescent lions – both male and female – may be evicted.[37]

Lions of both sexes may interact homosexually. Lions are shown to be involved in group homosexual and courtship activities; males will also head-rub and roll around with each other before simulating sex together.[38]

Health

Although adult lions have no natural predators, evidence suggests most die violently from attacks by humans or other lions.[39] Lions often inflict serious injuries on members of other prides they encounter in territorial disputes or members of the home pride when fighting at a kill.[40] Crippled lions and cubs may fall victim to hyenas and leopards or be trampled by buffalo or elephants. Careless lions may be maimed when hunting prey.[41]

Ticks commonly infest the ears, neck and groin regions of lions.[42] Adult forms of several species of the tapeworm genus *Taenia* have been isolated from lion intestines, having been ingested as larvae in antelope meat. Lions in

Figure 11: *Kenyan lions seeking refuge from*
flies by climbing a tree near Lake Nakuru

the Ngorongoro Crater were afflicted by an outbreak of stable fly (*Stomoxys calcitrans*) in 1962; this resulted in lions becoming emaciated and covered in bloody, bare patches. Lions sought unsuccessfully to evade the biting flies by climbing trees or crawling into hyena burrows; many perished or migrated and the local population dropped from 70 to 15 individuals. A more recent outbreak in 2001 killed six lions.

Lions, especially those in captivity, are vulnerable to the canine distemper virus (CDV), feline immunodeficiency virus (FIV) and feline infectious peritonitis (FIP). CDV is spread by domestic dogs and other carnivores; a 1994 outbreak in Serengeti National Park resulted in many lions developing neurological symptoms such as seizures. During the outbreak, several lions died from pneumonia and encephalitis. FIV, which is similar to HIV – while not known to adversely affect lions – is worrisome enough in its effect in domestic cats that the Species Survival Plan recommends systematic testing in captive lions. The virus occurs with high-to-endemic frequency in several wild lion populations but is mostly absent from Asiatic and Namibian lions.

Figure 12: *Head rubbing and licking are common social behaviours within a pride*

Communication

When resting, lion socialisation occurs through a number of behaviours; the animal's expressive movements are highly developed. The most common peaceful, tactile gestures are head rubbing and social licking,[43] which have been compared with grooming in primates.[44] Head rubbing – the nuzzling of the forehead, face and neck against another lion – appears to be a form of greeting and is seen often after an animal has been apart from others or after a fight or confrontation. Males tend to rub other males, while cubs and females rub females.[45] Social licking often occurs in tandem with head rubbing; it is generally mutual and the recipient appears to express pleasure. The head and neck are the most common parts of the body licked; this behaviour may have arisen out of utility because lions cannot lick these areas themselves.[46]

	Lion roar A captive lion in India roaring

Problems playing this file? See media help.

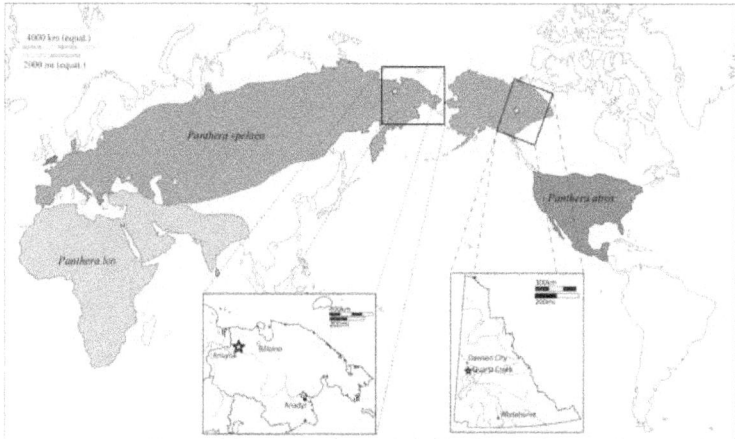

Figure 13: *The maximal range of lion species in the past: red
indicates Panthera spelaea, blue P. atrox, and green P. leo*

Lions have an array of facial expressions and body postures that serve as visual gestures.[47] A common facial expression is the "grimace face" or flehmen
response, which a lion makes when sniffing chemical signals and involves an
open mouth with bared teeth, raised muzzle, wrinkled nose closed eyes and
relaxed ears.[48] Lions also use chemical and visual marking; males will spray
and scrape plots of ground and objects within the territory.

The repertoire of vocalisations is also large; rather than discrete signals, variations in intensity and pitch appear to be central to communication. Most
lion vocalisations are variations of growling, snarling, miaowing and roaring.
Other sounds produced include purring, puffing, bleating and humming. Lions
tend to roar in a very characteristic manner starting with a few deep, long roars
that subside into a series of shorter ones. They most often roar at night; the
sound, which can be heard from a distance of 8 kilometres (5.0 mi), is used to
advertise the animal's presence.[49]

Distribution and habitat

The lion prefers grassy plains and savannahs, scrub bordering rivers and open
woodlands with bushes. It is absent from rainforest and rarely enters closed
forest. On Mount Elgon, the lion has been recorded up to an elevation of
3,600 m (11,800 ft) and close to the snow line on Mount Kenya. Lions occur
in savannah grasslands with scattered *Acacia* trees, which serve as shade.

Figure 14: *Two male, captive Asiatic lions in Sanjay Gandhi National Park, Mumbai*

In Africa, the range of the lion originally spanned most of the central rainforest zone and the Sahara desert.[50] In the 1960s, it became extinct in North Africa, except in the southern part of Sudan.

In Eurasia, the lion once ranged from Greece to India; Herodotus reported that lions had been common in Greece in 480 BC; they attacked the baggage camels of the Persian king Xerxes on his march through the country. Aristotle considered them rare by 300 BC, and by 100 AD, they had been extirpated. Until the 10th century, lions survived in the Caucasus, their last European outpost. The species was eradicated in Palestine by the Middle Ages, and from most of the rest of Asia after the arrival of readily available firearms in the 18th century. Between the late 19th and late 20th centuries, it became extinct in Southwest Asia. By the late 19th century, the lion had been extirpated in most of northern India and Turkey. The last live lion in Iran was sighted in 1942, about 65 km (40 mi) northwest of Dezful. The corpse of a lioness was found on the banks of the Karun river, Khūzestān Province, in 1944. There are no subsequent reliable reports from Iran.

The Asiatic lion now only survives in and around Gir Forest National Park in Gujarat, western India. Its habitat is a mixture of dry savannah forest and very dry, deciduous scrub forest.

Figure 15: *Black maned male lion, shot in the Sotik Plains, Kenya (May 1909)*

Conservation

In Africa

Most lions now live in East and Southern Africa; their numbers are rapidly decreasing, and fell by an estimated 30–50% each 20 years in the late half of the 20th century. The species is listed as Vulnerable on the IUCN Red List. In 1975, it was estimated that since the 1950s, lion numbers decreased by half to 200,000 or fewer.[51] Estimates of the African lion population range between 16,500 and 47,000 living in the wild in 2002–2004. Primary causes of the decline include disease and human interference. Habitat loss and conflicts with humans are considered to be the most significant threats to the species.

The Ewaso Lions Project protects lions in the Samburu National Reserve, Buffalo Springs National Reserve and Shaba National Reserve of the Ewaso Ng'iro ecosystem in northern Kenya. Outside these areas, the problems arising from lions' interaction with humans and their livestock usually results in the killing of the lions.

Zambia's Kafue National Park is a key refuge for lions where frequent, uncontrolled bushfires combined with hunting of lions and prey species limits the ability of the lion population to recover. When favourable habitat is inundated

Figure 16: *A male lion in Pendjari National Park, Benin.*
West African lions are considered to be critically endangered

in the wet season, lions expand home ranges and travel greater distances, and cub mortality is high.

In 2015, a population of up to 200 lions that was previously thought to have been extirpated was filmed in the Alatash National Park, Ethiopia, close to the Sudanese border.

The West African lion population is isolated from the one in Central Africa, with little or no exchange of breeding individuals. In 2015, it was estimated that this population consists of about 400 animals, including fewer than 250 mature individuals. They persist in three protected areas in the region, mostly in one population in the WAP protected area complex, shared by Benin, Burkina Faso and Niger. This population is listed as Critically Endangered. Field surveys in the WAP ecosystem revealed that lion occupancy is lowest in the W National Park, and higher in areas with permanent staff and thus better protection. A population occurs in Cameroon's Waza National Park, where between approximately 14 and 21 animals persisted as of 2009. In addition, 50 to 150 lions in are estimated to be present in Burkina Faso's Arly-Singou ecosystem. In 2015, an adult male lion and a female lion were sighted in Ghana's Mole National Park. These were the first sightings of lions in the country in 39 years.

In Gabon's Batéké Plateau National Park, a single male lion was repeatedly recorded by camera-traps between January 2015 and September 2017. Five hair samples from this lion were collected and compared with samples from

Figure 17: *Lion couple at Botlierskop Private Game Reserve in South Africa*

museum specimens that had been shot in the area in 1959. Genetic analysis showed the Batéké lion is closely related to lions killed in this region in the past. The samples grouped it with lion samples from Namibia and Botswana, raising the possibility that the Batéké lion either dispersed from a Southern African lion population or is a survivor of the ancestral Batéké population that was considered to be extinct since the late 1990s.

In the Republic of the Congo, Odzala-Kokoua National Park was considered a lion stronghold in the 1990s. By 2014, no lions were recorded in the protected area so the population is considered locally extinct. In the Democratic Republic of the Congo, there are about 150 lions in Garamba National Park, and 90 in Virunga National Park; he latter form a contiguous population with lions in Uganda. In 2010, the lion population in Uganda was estimated at 408 ± 46 individuals in three protected areas including Queen Elizabeth National Park. Little is known about lion distribution and population sizes in adjacent South Sudan. In Sudan, lions were reported in Southern Darfur and Southern Kordofan provinces in the 1980s.

In Asia

The last refuge of the Asiatic lion population is the 1,412 km^2 (545 sq mi) Gir Forest National Park and surrounding areas in the region of Saurashtra or Kathiawar Peninsula in Gujarat State, India. The population has risen from approximately 180 lions in 1974 to about 400 in 2010. It is geographically

Figure 18: *A lioness in Gir Forest National Park, India*

Figure 19: *A Male Lion at Bannargatta National Park, Bangalore, India*

isolated, which can lead to inbreeding and reduced genetic diversity. Since 2008, the Asiatic lion has been listed as Endangered on the IUCN Red List. By 2015, the population had grown to 523 individuals inhabiting an area of 7,000 km^2 (2,700 sq mi) in Saurashtra. The Asiatic Lion Census conducted in 2017 recorded about 650 individuals.

The presence of numerous human habitations close to the National Park results in conflict between lions, local people and their livestock. Some consider the presence of lions a benefit, as they keep populations of crop damaging herbivores in check. The establishment of a second, independent Asiatic lion population in Kuno Wildlife Sanctuary, located in Madhya Pradesh was planned but in 2017, the Asiatic Lion Reintroduction Project seemed unlikely to be implemented.

Captive breeding

Lions are included in the Species Survival Plan, a coordinated attempt by the Association of Zoos and Aquariums to increase its chances of survival. The plan was started in 1982 for the Asiatic lion, but was suspended when it was found that most Asiatic lions in North American zoos were not genetically pure, having been hybridised with African lions. The African lion plan started in 1993, and focused on the South African population, although there are difficulties in assessing the genetic diversity of captive lions because most individuals are of unknown origin, making the maintenance of genetic diversity a problem. Breeding programs need to note origins to avoid breeding different subspecies and thus reducing their conservation value. Several Asiatic-African lion crosses, however, have been bred.

The former popularity of the Barbary lion as a zoo animal means captive lions are likely descended from Barbary lion stock. This includes lions at Port Lympne Wild Animal Park in Kent, England, that allegedly descended from animals owned by the King of Morocco. Another eleven animals thought to be Barbary lions kept in Addis Ababa Zoo are descendants of animals owned by Emperor Haile Selassie. WildLink International in collaboration with Oxford University launched an ambitious International Barbary Lion Project with the aim of identifying and breeding Barbary lions in captivity for eventual reintroduction into a national park in the Atlas Mountains of Morocco.

Figure 20: *Lion cubs at Clifton Zoological Gardens, England, 1854*

Interactions with humans

In captivity

Lions are part of a group of exotic animals that have been central to zoo exhibits since the late 18th century; members of this group are invariably large vertebrates and include elephants, rhinoceroses, hippopotamuses, large primates and other big cats; zoos sought to gather as many of these species as possible.[52] Although many modern zoos are more selective about their exhibits, there are more than 1,000 African and 100 Asiatic lions in zoos and wildlife parks around the world. They are considered an ambassador species and are kept for tourism, education and conservation purposes. Lions can reach an age of over 20 years in captivity; Apollo, a resident lion of Honolulu Zoo in Honolulu, Hawaii, died at age 22 in August 2007. His two sisters, born in 1986, were still alive in August 2007.

At the ancient Egyptian cities of Taremu and Per-Bast were temples dedicated to the lion goddesses of Egypt, Sekhmet and Bast, and at Taremu there was a temple dedicated to the son of the deity Maahes the lion prince, where lions were kept and allowed to roam within the temple. The Greeks called the city *Leontopolis* ("City of Lions") and documented that practice. Lions were kept and bred by Assyrian kings as early as 850 BC, and Alexander the Great was

Figure 21: *Guided Tour with lions, Botlierskop Game Reserve in South Africa*

said to have been presented with tame lions by the Malhi of northern India. In Ancient Rome, lions were kept by emperors to take part in the gladiator arenas or were used for executions (see bestiarii, damnatio ad bestias, and venatio). Roman notables including Sulla, Pompey and Julius Caesar often ordered the mass slaughter of hundreds of lions at a time. In India, lions were tamed by Indian princes. Marco Polo reported that Kublai Khan kept lions.[53]

The first European "zoos" spread among noble and royal families in the 13th century, and until the 17th century were called seraglios; at that time they came to be called menageries, an extension of the cabinet of curiosities. They spread from France and Italy during the Renaissance to the rest of Europe.[54] In England, although the seraglio tradition was less developed, lions were kept at the Tower of London in a seraglio established by King John in the 13th century;[55] this was probably stocked with animals from an earlier menagerie started in 1125 by Henry I at his hunting lodge in Woodstock, Oxfordshire, where according to William of Malmesbury lions had been stocked.[56]

Seraglios served as expressions of the nobility's power and wealth; animals – particularly big cats and elephants – symbolised power and were pitted against each other or domesticated animals in fights. By extension, menageries and seraglios served as demonstrations of the dominance of humanity over nature; the defeat of such natural "lords" by a cow in 1682 astonished spectators and the flight of an elephant before a rhinoceros drew jeers. The frequency of such fights slowly declined in the 17th century with the spread of menageries and

Figure 22: *Albrecht Dürer, lions sketch. (c. 1520)*

their appropriation by commoners. The tradition of keeping big cats as pets lasted into the 19th century, at which time it was seen as highly eccentric.[57]

The presence of lions at the Tower of London was intermittent, being restocked when a monarch or his consort, such as Margaret of Anjou the wife of Henry VI, either sought or were given animals. Records indicate animals in the Tower of London were kept in poor conditions in the 17th century, in contrast to more open conditions in Florence at the time.[58] The menagerie was open to the public by the 18th century; admission was a sum of three half-pence or the supply of a cat or dog for feeding to the lions.[59] A rival menagerie at the Exeter Exchange also exhibited lions until the early 19th century.[60] The Tower menagerie was closed by William IV, and the animals were transferred to London Zoo, which opened to the public on 27 April 1828.[61]

The trade in wild animals flourished alongside improved colonial trade of the 19th century; lions were considered fairly common and inexpensive. Although they would barter higher than tigers, they were less costly than larger or more difficult-to-transport animals such as the giraffe and hippopotamus, and much less than giant pandas.[62] Like other animals, lions were seen as little more than a natural, boundless commodity that was mercilessly exploited with terrible losses in capture and transportation.[63]

Lions were kept in cramped and squalid conditions at London Zoo until a larger lion house with roomier cages was built in the 1870s.[64] Further changes took

Figure 23: *Lion at Melbourne Zoo enjoying
an elevated grassy area with some tree shelter*

place in the early 20th century when Carl Hagenbeck designed enclosures with
concrete "rocks", more open space and a moat instead of bars, more closely re-
sembling a natural habitat. Hagenbeck designed lion enclosures for both Melbourne Zoo and Sydney's Taronga Zoo; although his designs were popular, the
use of bars and caged enclosures prevailed in many zoos until the 1960s.[65] In
the late 20th century, larger, more natural enclosures and the use of wire mesh
or laminated glass instead of lowered dens allowed visitors to come closer than
ever to the animals; some attractions such as the Cat Forest/Lion Overlook of
Oklahoma City Zoological Park placed the den on ground level, higher than
visitors.

Hunting, baiting and taming

Lion hunting has occurred since ancient times and was often a royal pastime.
The earliest surviving record of lion hunting is an ancient Egyptian inscription
dated circa 1380 BC that mentions Pharaoh Amenhotep III killing 102 lions
"with his own arrows" during the first ten years of his rule. The Assyrians
would release captive lions in a reserved space for the king to hunt; this event
would be watched by spectators as the king and his men, on horseback or
chariots, killed the lions with arrows and spears. Lions were also hunted during
the Mughal Empire, where Emperor Jahangir is said to have excelled at it.

Figure 24: *Bas-relief of a wounded lion from Nineveh, Mesopotamia, during the Neo-Assyrian period (c. 645-635 BC)*

Royal hunting of lions was intended to demonstrate the power of the king over nature.[66]

The Maasai people have traditionally viewed the killing of lions as a rite of passage. Historically, lions were hunted by individuals, however, due to reduced lion populations, elders discourage solo lion hunts. During the European colonisation of Africa in the 19th century, the hunting of lions was encouraged because they were considered as vermin and lion hides fetched £1 each.[67] The widely reproduced imagery of the heroic hunter chasing lions would dominate a large part of the century.[68] Explorers and hunters exploited a popular Manichean division of animals into "good" and "evil" to add thrilling value to their adventures, casting themselves as heroic figures. This resulted in big cats being always suspected of being man-eaters, representing "both the fear of nature and the satisfaction of having overcome it".[69] Trophy hunting of lions in recent years has been met with controversy; the killing of Cecil the lion in mid-2015 by an American tourist created a significant international backlash against the hunter and of the practice of hunting lions.

Lion-baiting is a blood sport involving the baiting of lions in combat with other animals, usually dogs. Records of it exist in ancient times through until the seventeenth century. It was finally banned in Vienna by 1800 and England in 1835.

Figure 25: *Nineteenth-century etching of a lion tamer in a cage of lions and tigers*

Lion taming refers to the practice of taming lions for entertainment, either as part of an established circus or as an individual act such as Siegfried & Roy. The term is also often used for the taming and display of other big cats such as tigers, leopards and cougars. The practice began in the early 19th century by Frenchman Henri Martin and American Isaac Van Amburgh, who both toured widely and whose techniques were copied by a number of followers. Van Amburgh performed before Queen Victoria in 1838 when he toured Great Britain. Martin composed a pantomime titled *Les Lions de Mysore* ("the lions of Mysore"), an idea that Amburgh quickly borrowed. These acts eclipsed equestrianism acts as the central display of circus shows and entered public consciousness in the early 20th century with cinema. In demonstrating the superiority of human over animal, lion taming served a purpose similar to animal fights of previous centuries.[70] The ultimate proof of a tamer's dominance and control over a lion is demonstrated by the placing of the tamer's head in the lion's mouth. The now-iconic lion tamer's chair was possibly first used by American Clyde Beatty (1903–1965).

Figure 26: *The Tsavo Man-Eaters on display in the Field Museum of Natural History in Chicago, Illinois.*

Man-eating

Lions do not usually hunt humans but some – usually males – seem to seek them out. One well-publicised case is the Tsavo maneaters; in 1898, 28 officially recorded railway workers building the Kenya-Uganda Railway were taken by lions over nine months during the construction of a bridge over the Tsavo River in Kenya. The hunter who killed the lions wrote a book detailing the animals' predatory behaviour; they were larger than normal and lacked manes, and one seemed to suffer from tooth decay. The infirmity theory, including tooth decay, is not favoured by all researchers; an analysis of teeth and jaws of man-eating lions in museum collections suggests that while tooth decay may explain some incidents, prey depletion in human-dominated areas is a more likely cause of lion predation on humans.

In their analysis of man-eating – including the Tsavo incident – Kerbis Peterhans and Gnoske acknowledge that sick or injured animals may be more prone to man-eating but that the behaviour is "not unusual, nor necessarily 'aberrant'" where the opportunity exists; if inducements such as access to livestock or human corpses are present, lions will regularly prey upon human beings. The authors note the relationship is well-attested among other pantherines and primates in the fossil record.

The lion's proclivity for man-eating has been systematically examined. American and Tanzanian scientists report that man-eating behaviour in rural areas of Tanzania increased greatly from 1990 to 2005. At least 563 villagers were attacked and many eaten over this period – a number far exceeding the Tsavo attacks. The incidents occurred near Selous National Park in Rufiji District and in Lindi Province near the Mozambican border. While the expansion of villages into bush country is one concern, the authors argue conservation policy must mitigate the danger because in this case, conservation contributes directly to human deaths. Cases in Lindi in which lions seize humans from the centres of substantial villages have been documented. Another study of 1,000 people attacked by lions in southern Tanzania between 1988 and 2009 found that the weeks following the full moon, when there was less moonlight, were a strong indicator of increased night-time attacks on people.

According to Robert R. Frump, Mozambican refugees regularly crossing Kruger National Park, South Africa, at night are attacked and eaten by lions; park officials have said man-eating is a problem there. Frump said thousands may have been killed in the decades after apartheid sealed the park and forced refugees to cross the park at night. For nearly a century before the border was sealed, Mozambicans had regularly crossed the park in daytime with little harm.

Packer estimates between 200 and 400 Tanzanians are killed each year by wild animals and that lions are thought to kill at least 70 of these. According to Packer between 1990 and 2004, lions attacked 815 people in Tanzania and killed 563. Packer and Ikanda are among the few conservationists who believe western conservation efforts must take account of these matters because of ethical concerns about human life and the long-term success of conservation efforts and lion preservation.

A man-eating lion was killed by game scouts in Southern Tanzania in April 2004. It is believed to have killed and eaten at least 35 people in a series of incidents covering several villages in the coastal Rufiji Delta region. Dr Rolf D. Baldus, the GTZ wildlife programme coordinator, said it was likely that the lion preyed on humans because it had a large abscess beneath a cracked molar and wrote, "This lion probably experienced a lot of pain, particularly when it was chewing". As in other cases this lion was large, lacked a mane, and had a tooth problem.

The "All-Africa" record of man-eating generally is considered to be a collection of incidents between the early 1930s and the late 1940s in modern-day Tanzania inflicted by a pride known as the "Njombe lions". Game warden and hunter George Rushby eventually dispatched the pride, which over three generations is thought to have killed and eaten 1,500 to 2,000 people in Njombe district.

Sometimes, Asiatic lions may become man-eaters. The area of the Gir sanctuary is now insufficient to sustain their large number and lions have moved

Figure 27: *Upper Paleolithic cave painting depicting lions, found in the Chauvet Cave, France*

outside it, making them a potential threat to people in and around the park. Two attacks on humans were reported in 2012 in an area about 50–60 km (31–37 mi) from the sanctuary.

Cultural significance

The lion is one of the most widely recognised animal symbols in human culture. It has been extensively depicted in sculptures and paintings, on national flags, and in contemporary films and literature. It appeared as a symbol for strength and nobility in cultures across Europe, Asia and Africa, despite incidents of attacks on people. The lion has been depicted as "king of the jungle" and "king of beasts", and thus became a popular symbol for royalty and stateliness.

Depictions of lions are known from the Upper Paleolithic period. Carvings and paintings of lions discovered in the Lascaux and Chauvet Caves in France have been dated to 15,000 to 17,000 years old.[71] A lioness-headed ivory carving found in Vogelherd cave in the Swabian Alb, south-west Germany, is dubbed *Löwenmensch* (lion-human) in German. The sculpture has been dated to least 32,000 years old – and as early as 40,000 years ago –[72] and originated from the Aurignacian culture.

Figure 28: *Granite statue of the Egyptian goddess Sekhmet from the Luxor Temple, dated 1403–1365 BC, exhibited in the National Museum of Denmark*

Africa

The ancient Egyptians portrayed several of their war deities as lionesses, which they revered as fierce hunters. Egyptian deities associated with lions include: Bast, Mafdet, Menhit, Pakhet, Sekhmet, Tefnut and the Sphinx. In Egypt, the avenging goddess Sekhmet, represented as a lioness, symbolized the heat of the sun. The lion was also believed to act as a guide to the underworld, through which the sun was believed to pass each night. The presence of lion-footed tombs found in Egypt and images of mummies carried on the backs of lions suggests this close association of the lions with the underworld. Partly mummified lions were excavated at the necropolis Umm El Qa'ab in a tomb of Hor-Aha, and at Saqqara in the tomb of Maïa.

In Sub-Saharan Africa, cultural views of the lion have varied by region. In some cultures, the lion symbolises power and royalty, and some rulers had the word "lion" in their nickname. For example, Marijata of the Mali Empire was given the name "Lion of Mali". Njaay, the founder of the Waalo kingdom, is said to have been raised by lions and returned to his people part-lion to unite them using the knowledge he learned from the lions. In parts of West Africa, to be compared with a lion was considered to be a great compliment. Lions were considered the top class in these cultures' social hierarchies. In more

Figure 29: *Daniel in the lions' den is an account in Daniel 6 in the Bible*

heavily forested areas where lions were rare, the leopard represented the top of the hierarchy.[73]

In parts of West and East Africa, the lion is associated with healing and is regarded as the link between seers and the supernatural. In other East African traditions, the lion is the symbol of laziness. In many folktales, lions are portrayed as having low intelligence and are easily tricked by other animals. Although lions were commonly used in stories, proverbs and dances, they rarely featured in visual arts.

Near East

The lion was a prominent symbol in ancient Mesopotamia from Sumer up to Assyrian and Babylonian times, where it was strongly associated with kingship. Lions were among the major symbols of the goddess Inanna/Ishtar. The Lion of Babylon was the foremost symbol of the Babylonian Empire. The *Lion Hunt of Ashurbanipal* is a famous sequence of Assyrian palace reliefs from c. 640 BC, now in the British Museum. In Meopotamia, the lion was linked with the fertility goddess Ishtar and the supreme Mesopotamian god Marduk. The theme of the royal lion hunt, a common motif in the early iconography in West Asia, symbolized death and resurrection; the continuation of life was ensured by the killing of a god-like animal. In some stone reliefs depicting the Royal hunt of lions, the lion's divinity and courage are equated with the divinity and courage of the king.

Figure 30: *Lion Capital of Ashoka, Sanchi, M. P., India.*

The lion is the biblical emblem of the tribe of Judah and the later Kingdom of Judah. Lions are frequently mentioned in the Bible; notably in the Book of Daniel in which the eponymous hero refuses to worship King Darius and is forced to sleep in the lions' den where he is miraculously unharmed (Dan 6[74]). In the Book of Judges, Samson kills a lion as he travels to visit a Philistine woman.(Judg 14[75]). The power and ferocity of the lion is invoked when describing the anger of God (Amos 3:4–8[76], Lam 3:10[77]) and the menace of Israel's enemies (Psm 17:12[78], Jer 2:30[79]) and Satan (1 Pet 5:8[80]). The book of Isaiah uses the imagery of a lion laying with a calf and child, and eating straw to portray the harmony of creation (Isa 11:6–7[81]). In the Book of Revelation, a lion, an ox, a man and an eagle are seen on a heavenly throne in John's vision;(Rev 4:7[82]) the early Christian Church used this image to symbolise the four gospels, the lion symbolising the Gospel of Mark.

Far East

In the Puranic texts of Hinduism, Narasimha ("man-lion") a half-lion, half-man incarnation or avatar of Vishnu, is worshipped by his devotees and saved the child devotee Prahlada from his father, the evil demon king Hiranyaka-shipu; Vishnu takes the form of half-man, half-lion] creature in Narasimha, where he has a human torso and lower body, and a lion-like face and claws. Singh is an ancient Indian vedic name meaning "lion", dating back over 2,000

Figure 31: *A Chinese guardian lion outside Yonghe Temple, Beijing*

years in ancient India. It was originally used only by Rajputs, a Hindu Ksha-triya or military caste. After the birth of the Khalsa brotherhood in 1699, the Sikhs also adopted the name "Singh" due to the wishes of Guru Gobind Singh. Along with millions of Hindu Rajputs today, it is also used by over 20 million Sikhs worldwide.

The Asiatic lion is found as an emblem on numerous flags and coats of arms across Asia, including on the National Emblem of India. The Asiatic lion is also symbolic for the Sinhalese, Sri Lanka's ethnic majority; the term derived from the Indo-Aryan *Sinhala*, meaning the "lion people" or "people with lion blood", while a sword-wielding lion is the central figure on the national flag of Sri Lanka.

The Asiatic lion is a common motif in Chinese art; it was first used in art dur-ing the late Spring and Autumn period (fifth or sixth century BC) and became more popular during the Han Dynasty (206 BC – AD 220) when imperial guardian lions started to be placed in front of imperial palaces for protection. Because lions have never been native to China, early depictions were some-what unrealistic; after the introduction of Buddhist art to China in the Tang Dynasty after the sixth century AD, lions were usually depicted wingless with shorter, thicker bodies and curly manes. The lion dance is a traditional dance in Chinese culture in which performers in lion costumes mimic a lion's move-ments, often with musical accompaniment from cymbals, drums and gongs.

Figure 32: *Heracles slaying the Nemean lion. Detail of a Roman mosaic from Llíria (Spain).*

They are performed at Chinese New Year, the August Moon Festival and other celebratory occasions for good luck.

Singapore derives its name from the Malay words *singa* (lion) and *pora* (city/fortress), which in turn is from the Tamil-Sanskrit சிங்க *singa* सिंह *siṃha* and पुर பुர *pura*, which is cognate to the Greek πόλις, *pólis*. According to the Malay Annals, this name was given by a fourteenth-century Sumatran Malay prince Sang Nila Utama, who, on alighting the island after a thunderstorm, spotted an auspicious beast that appeared to be a lion on the shore.

Europe

Lion-headed figures and amulets were excavated in tombs in the Greek islands of Crete, Euboea, Rhodes, Paros and Chios. They are associated with the Egyptian deity Sekhmet and date to the early Iron Age between the 9th and 6th centuries BC.

The lion is featured in several of Aesop's fables, which were written in the sixth century BC. The Nemean lion was symbolic in ancient Greece and Rome, represented as the constellation and zodiac sign Leo, and described in mythology, where its skin was borne by the hero Heracles. Myths which have a hero killing

Figure 33: *Coat of arms of England*
with significantly inaccurate anatomy

a lion, such as the one in which Herakles slays the Nemean lion, symbolize victory over death. Similarly the wearing of lion skin such as the lion skin worn by Herackles also symbolizes victory over death.

"Lion" was the nickname of several medieval warrior-rulers with a reputation for bravery, such as the English King Richard the Lionheart, Henry the Lion, (German: *Heinrich der Löwe*), Duke of Saxony, William the Lion, King of Scotland, and Robert III of Flanders was nicknamed "The Lion of Flanders" – a major Flemish national icon.

Lions are frequently depicted on coats of arms, either as a device on shields or as supporters, but the lioness is used much less frequently. The formal language of heraldry, called blazon, employs French terms to describe the images precisely. Such descriptions specify whether lions or other creatures are "rampant" (rearing) or "passant" (crouching).

Modern culture

The lion is used as a symbol of sporting teams, from national association football teams such as England, Scotland and Singapore to famous clubs such as the Detroit Lions of the NFL, Chelsea and Aston Villa, a team of the English

Premier League, and by the Premiership itself, Eintracht Braunschweig of the Bundesliga, and many smaller clubs around the world.

Lions continue to appear in modern literature as characters including the messianic Aslan in *The Lion, the Witch and the Wardrobe* and following books from The Chronicles of Narnia series written by C. S. Lewis, and the comedic Cowardly Lion in *The Wonderful Wizard of Oz*. Lion synmbolism was used from the advent of cinema; one of the most iconic and widely recognised lions is Leo, which has been the mascot for Metro-Goldwyn-Mayer (MGM) studios since the 1920s. The 1960s saw the appearance of the Kenyan lioness Elsa in the movie *Born Free*, which is based on the factual book of the same title. The lion's role as king of the beasts has been used in cartoons, such as the 1994 Disney animated feature film *The Lion King*.

References

Cited texts

<templatestyles src="Refbegin/styles.css" />

- Baratay, Eric; Hardouin-Fugier, Elisabeth (2002). *Zoo: a history of zoological gardens in the West*. London: Reaktion Books. ISBN 978-1-86189-111-2.<templatestyles src="Module:Citation/CS1/styles.css"></templatestyles>
- Blunt, Wilfred (1975). *The Ark in the Park: The Zoo in the Nineteenth Century*. London: Hamish Hamilton. ISBN 978-0-241-89331-9.<templatestyles src="Module:Citation/CS1/styles.css"></templatestyles>
- de Courcy, Catherine (1995). *The Zoo Story*. Ringwood, Victoria: Penguin Books. ISBN 978-0-14-023919-5.<templatestyles src="Module:Citation/CS1/styles.css"></templatestyles>
- Denis-Hoot, Christine; Denis-Hoot, Michel (2002). *The Art of Being a Lion*. Freidman/Fairfax. ISBN 978-1-58663-707-1.<templatestyles src="Module:Citation/CS1/styles.css"></templatestyles>
- Jackson, Deirdre (2010). *Lion*. Reaktion Books. ISBN 978-1861896551.<templatestyles src="Module:Citation/CS1/styles.css"></templatestyles>
- Schaller, George B. (1972). *The Serengeti lion: A study of predator–prey relations*. Chicago: University of Chicago Press. ISBN 978-0-226-73639-6.<templatestyles src="Module:Citation/CS1/styles.css"></templatestyles>
- Scott, Jonathan; Scott, Angela (2002). *Big Cat Diary: Lion*. Harper Collins. ISBN 978-0-00-714666-6.<templatestyles src="Module:Citation/CS1/styles.css"></templatestyles>

External links

| ሃዋ፝Ꭽ
ᴧᎽᏑ
ᵼ᾽ᎦᎥ | Look up *lion* in Wiktionary, the free dictionary. |

| | Wikispecies has information related to *Lion* |

| | Wikisource has the text of the 1921 *Collier's Encyclopedia* article *Lion*. |

| | Wikimedia Commons has media related to *Lion*. |

- Species portrait Lion; IUCN/SSC Cat Specialist Group[83]
- "Lion Conservation Fund"[84].<templatestyles src="Module:Citation/CS1/styles.css"></templatestyles> Example of a fund and its projects about the research and conservation of the lion.
- A lion that traveled[85] almost 1,300 km (810 mi) between Angola and Namibia

Appendix

References

[1] Schaller, pp. 28–30.
[2] Schaller, p. 122.
[3] Schaller, pp. 120–21.
[4] Schaller, p. 33.
[5] Schaller, p. 37.
[6] Schaller, p. 39.
[7] Schaller, p. 44.
[8] Schaller, p. 34–35.
[9] Schaller, pp. 52–54.
[10] Join the Pride http://www.lionconservationfund.org/lion_adopt.html. Lion Conservation Fund. Retrieved on 31 July 2013.
[11] Schaller, p. 195.
[12] Schaller, pp. 220–221.
[13] Denis-Hoot, 188.
[14]
[15] Schaller, p. 153.
[16] Schaller, p. 259.
[17] Schaller, p. 248.
[18] Schaller, pp. 247–48.
[19] Schaller, p. 237.
[20] Schaller, p. 133.
[21] Schaller, p. 276.
[22]
[23] Schaller, p. 213.
[24] Schaller, p. 272.
[25] Schaller, pp. 273–74.
[26] Denis-Hoot, 198.
[27] Schaller, p. 293.
[28] Schaller, p. 188.
[29] Schaller, p. 29.
[30] Schaller, p. 174.
[31] Schramm, Ralph Dee, Michael B. Briggs, and Jerry J. Reeves. " Spontaneous and induced ovulation in the lion (Panthera leo) https://onlinelibrary.wiley.com/doi/abs/10.1002/zoo. 1430130403." Zoo Biology 13.4 (1994): 301-307.
[32] Schaller, p. 142.
[33] Scott, p. 45.
[34] Schaller, p. 143.
[35] Schaller, p. 147-49.
[36] Scott, p. 46.
[37] Scott, p. 68.
[38] Schaller, p. 137.
[39] Schaller, p. 183.
[40] Schaller, pp. 188–89.
[41] Schaller, pp. 189–90.
[42] Schaller, p. 184.
[43] Schaller, p. 85.
[44] (2007 edition: 0-202-30826-X)
[45] Schaller, pp. 85–88.
[46] Schaller, pp. 88–91.
[47] Schaller, pp. 103–117.

[48] Schaller, p. 95.
[49]

[50] Schaller, p. 5.
[51] Myers, N. (1975). The silent savannahs. International Wildlife 5 (5): 5–10.
[52] de Courcy, p. 81-82.
[53] Baratay & Hardouin-Fugier, p. 17.
[54] Baratay & Hardouin-Fugier, pp. 19–21, 42.
[55] Baratay & Hardouin-Fugier, p. 20.
[56] Blunt, p. 15.
[57] Baratay & Hardouin-Fugier, pp. 24–28.
[58] Blunt, p. 16.
[59] Blunt, p. 17.
[60] de Courcy, pp. 8–9.
[61] Blunt, p. 32.
[62] Baratay & Hardouin-Fugier, p. 122.
[63] Baratay & Hardouin-Fugier, pp. 114, 117.
[64] Blunt, p. 208.
[65] de Courcy, p. 69.
[66] Jackson, p. 156–159.
[67] Jackson, p. 166.
[68] Baratay & Hardouin-Fugier, p. 113.
[69] Baratay & Hardouin-Fugier, pp. 173, 180–83.
[70]

[71] Leroi-Gourhan, A., Allain J. (1979). Lascaux inconnu. XXIIe supplement à "Gallia Préhistoire". Paris.
[72] Bailey, M. (2013). Ice Age Lion Man is world's earliest figurative sculpture. http://www.theartnewspaper.com/articles/Ice-Age-iLion-Mani-is-worlds-earliest-figurative-sculpture/28595 The Art Newspaper, 31 January2013.
[73] Jackson, p. 119.
[74] https://www.biblegateway.com/passage/?search=Dan+6&version=NRSV
[75] https://www.biblegateway.com/passage/?search=Judg+14&version=NRSV
[76] https://www.biblegateway.com/passage/?search=Amos+3%3A4%E2%80%938&version=NRSV
[77] https://www.biblegateway.com/passage/?search=Lam+3%3A10&version=NRSV
[78] https://www.biblegateway.com/passage/?search=Psm+17%3A12&version=22%3A21
[79] https://www.biblegateway.com/passage/?search=Jer+2%3A30&version=5%3A6
[80] https://www.biblegateway.com/passage/?search=1+Pet+5%3A8&version=NRSV
[81] https://www.biblegateway.com/passage/?search=Isa+11%3A6%E2%80%937&version=NRSV
[82] https://www.biblegateway.com/passage/?search=Rev+4%3A7&version=NRSV
[83] http://www.catsg.org/index.php?id=108
[84] http://www.lionconservationfund.org/
[85] http://www.theportugalnews.com/news/rare-desert-lion-killed-in-angola-after-supplying-unprecedented-data/32633

Article Sources and Contributors

The sources listed for each article provide more detailed licensing information including the copyright status, the copyright owner, and the license conditions.

Lion *Source:* https://en.wikipedia.org/w/index.php?oldid=865247057 *License:* Creative Commons Attribution-Share Alike 3.0 *Contributors:* 2dk, 83d40m, Aliwal2012, Altaileopard, Apokryltaros, Axl, BD2412, Baffle gab1978, BhagyaMani, Biologytx, Casliber, EditerBoyGudAtSpel, EdmundT, Headbomb, Holdoffhunger, Ji.rodriguezmarin, Jordanmiller335, Jts1882, Kailash29792, L293D, Laser brain, Leo1pard, LittleJerry, MaoGo, Mcelite, Monsieur X, Mydreamsparrow, Narky Blert, Natg 19, Ninjalectual, Nutster, Olga Ernst, PSR B1937+21, Palindromedairy, Pbrower2a, Plutoniumjesus, Punetor i Rregullt5, RAFiFan, Rr603689, SHM198, Saberrex-Strongheart, SilverTiger12, Sumanuil, Surtsicna, WolfmanSF 1

Image Sources, Licenses and Contributors

The sources listed for each image provide more detailed licensing information including the copyright status, the copyright owner, and the license conditions.

Image *Source:* https://en.wikipedia.org/w/index.php?title=File:Padlock-silver.svg *Contributors:* AzaToth, BotMultichill, BotMultichillT, Gurch, Jarekt, Kallerna, Multichill, Perhelion, Rd232, Riana, Sarang, Siebrand, Steinsplitter, 4 anonymous edits ... 1
Image *Source:* https://en.wikipedia.org/w/index.php?title=File:Cscr-featured.svg *License:* GNU Lesser General Public License *Contributors:* Anomie ... 1
Image *Source:* https://en.wikipedia.org/w/index.php?title=File:Lion_waiting_in_Namibia.jpg *License:* Creative Commons Attribution 2.0 *Contributors:* Kevin Pluck ... 1
Image *Source:* https://en.wikipedia.org/w/index.php?title=File:Okonjima_Lioness.jpg *License:* GNU Free Documentation License *Contributors:* Falense ... 1
Image *Source:* https://en.wikipedia.org/w/index.php?title=File:Status_iucn3.1_VU.svg *Contributors:* Pengo, Pzgulyas ... 1
Image *Source:* https://en.wikipedia.org/w/index.php?title=File:Red_Pencil_Icon.png *License:* Creative Commons Zero *Contributors:* User:Peter coxhead ... 1
Image *Source:* https://en.wikipedia.org/w/index.php?title=File:Dagger-14-plain.png *License:* Creative Commons Zero *Contributors:* RexxS ... 2
Image *Source:* https://en.wikipedia.org/w/index.php?title=File:Lion_distribution.png *License:* Public domain *Contributors:* Tommyknocker (talk) 2
Figure 1 *Source:* https://en.wikipedia.org/w/index.php?title=File:Two_cladograms_for_Panthera.svg *License:* Creative Commons Attribution-Sharealike 3.0 *Contributors:* User:Sainsf, User:Zirguezi ... 4
Figure 2 *Source:* https://en.wikipedia.org/w/index.php?title=File:Hoehlenloewe_CaveLion_hharder.jpg *License:* Public Domain *Contributors:* Heinrich Harder (1858-1935) ... 5
Figure 3 *Source:* https://en.wikipedia.org/w/index.php?title=File:Lion_subspecies_distribution3.png *Contributors:* Altaileopard, Leo1pard ... 7
Figure 4 *Source:* https://en.wikipedia.org/w/index.php?title=File:Panthera_Atrox.jpg *License:* Creative Commons Attribution-Sharealike 2.0 *Contributors:* Claire H. from New York City, USA ... 8
Figure 5 *Source:* https://en.wikipedia.org/w/index.php?title=File:Iranian_-_Cylinder_Seal_with_a_Lion_Hunt_-_Walters_42797.jpg *Contributors:* Daderot, File Upload Bot (Kaldari), JMCC1, Johnbod, Mmcannis∼commonswiki, Zykasaa ... 9
Image *Source:* https://en.wikipedia.org/w/index.php?title=File:Asiatischer_Loewe_Panthera_leo_persica_Tiergarten_Nuernberg-21.jpg *Contributors:* Rufus46 ... 11
Image *Source:* https://en.wikipedia.org/w/index.php?title=File:Maneless_lion_from_Tsavo_East_National_Park.png *License:* Creative Commons Attribution-ShareAlike 3.0 Unported *Contributors:* Mgiganteus ... 11
Figure 6 *Source:* https://en.wikipedia.org/w/index.php?title=File:White_Lion.jpg *License:* Creative Commons Attribution 2.5 *Contributors:* Stano Novak ... 12
Figure 7 *Source:* https://en.wikipedia.org/w/index.php?title=File:Panthera_leo_stretching_(Etosha,_2012).jpg *License:* Creative Commons Attribution-Sharealike 3.0 *Contributors:* User:Yathin sk ... 13
Image *Source:* https://en.wikipedia.org/w/index.php?title=File:Pride_of_lions.JPG *License:* Public Domain *Contributors:* Rick marin (personal photograph taken myself) ... 13
Image *Source:* https://en.wikipedia.org/w/index.php?title=File:Lions_Family_Portrait_Masai_Mara.jpg *License:* Creative Commons Attribution-Sharealike 3.0 *Contributors:* User:Benh ... 14
Image *Source:* https://en.wikipedia.org/w/index.php?title=File:Tree-climbing_lions_(Panthera_leo).jpg *Contributors:* Alexis Jazz, Charlesjsharp, Leo1pard, 1 anonymous edits ... 14
Image *Source:* https://en.wikipedia.org/w/index.php?title=File:Panthera_leo_-zoo_-yawning-8a.jpg *License:* Creative Commons Attribution 2.0 *Contributors:* AbZahri AbAzizis from Kuala Lumpur, Malaysia ... 16
Image *Source:* https://en.wikipedia.org/w/index.php?title=File:Serengeti_Lion_Running_saturated.jpg *License:* Creative Commons Attribution-Sharealike 2.5 *Contributors:* Taken by Schuyler Shepherd (Ununuium272). Contrast and saturation edited by norro ... 16
Image *Source:* https://en.wikipedia.org/w/index.php?title=File:Lions_taking_down_cape_buffalo.jpg *License:* Creative Commons Attribution-Sharealike 3.0 *Contributors:* Caelio ... 16
Image *Source:* https://en.wikipedia.org/w/index.php?title=File:Lion_and_eland.jpg *License:* Public domain *Contributors:* Abyssal, Ghouston, Gunnex, Kersti Nebelsiek, OgreBot 2, Suidpunt, 1 anonymous edits ... 16
Figure 8 *Source:* https://en.wikipedia.org/w/index.php?title=File:Hyenas_Fight_Against_Lions_Over_a_Kill_HD_10.png *Contributors:* Dyolf77, Kersti Nebelsiek, Leo1pard, Mariomassone ... 19
Figure 9 *Source:* https://en.wikipedia.org/w/index.php?title=File:Lioness_vs_Leopard_9_July_2016_Latest_Sightings_1.png *Contributors:* INeverCry, Leo1pard, Mariomassone ... 20
Image *Source:* https://en.wikipedia.org/w/index.php?title=File:Panthera_leo_massaica_mating.jpg *License:* Creative Commons Attribution 2.0 *Contributors:* BhagyaMani, Leo1pard, Pan American-Grace, Rubin16, ცრინვალის რეგიონი ... 20
Image *Source:* https://en.wikipedia.org/w/index.php?title=File:Lion_cub,_Masai_Mara,_Kenya.jpg *License:* Creative Commons Attribution-Sharealike 2.0 *Contributors:* Paul Mannix ... 20
Figure 10 *Source:* https://en.wikipedia.org/w/index.php?title=File:Lion_Cubs_Phinda_2011.ogv *License:* Creative Commons Zero *Contributors:* GalliasM ... 22
Figure 11 *Source:* https://en.wikipedia.org/w/index.php?title=File:Lake-Nakuru-Lions-in-Tree.JPG *License:* Creative Commons Attribution-Sharealike 3.0 *Contributors:* User:Uspn ... 23
Figure 12 *Source:* https://en.wikipedia.org/w/index.php?title=File:Lion_cub_with_mother.jpg *License:* Creative Commons Attribution-Sharealike 2.0 *Contributors:* Abujoy, AnonEMouse, Ark, Badseed, Clayoquot, FlickreviewR, Hohum, SunOfErat, Winterkind, Zanaq, 1 anonymous edits ... 24
Image *Source:* https://en.wikipedia.org/w/index.php?title=File:Gnome-mime-sound-openclipart.svg *Contributors:* User:Eubulides ... 24
Figure 13 *Source:* https://en.wikipedia.org/w/index.php?title=File:Cave_lion_range.png *License:* Creative Commons Attribution-Sharealike 3.0 *Contributors:* Archaeodontosaurus, FunkMonk, Ruff tuff cream puff, William Harris, ديفيد عادل وهبة خليل 2 ... 25
Figure 14 *Source:* https://en.wikipedia.org/w/index.php?title=File:India_Animals.jpg *License:* Creative Commons Attribution-Sharealike 2.0 *Contributors:* supersujit ... 26
Figure 15 *Source:* https://en.wikipedia.org/w/index.php?title=File:The_Big_Game_of_Africa_(1910)_-_Male_lion_Sotik_Plains_May_1909.png *License:* Public Domain *Contributors:* Animalparty, BhagyaMani, Leo1pard, Mariomassone ... 27
Figure 16 *Source:* https://en.wikipedia.org/w/index.php?title=File:West_African_male_lion.jpg *License:* Creative Commons Attribution-Sharealike 3.0 *Contributors:* User:Jvdvoorde ... 28
Figure 17 *Source:* https://en.wikipedia.org/w/index.php?title=File:Lion_couple,_Botlierskop_(South_Africa).jpg *Contributors:* User:Olga Ernst 29
Figure 18 *Source:* https://en.wikipedia.org/w/index.php?title=File:Lion_Gir.jpg *License:* Creative Commons Attribution 2.0 *Contributors:* Rupal Vaidya from Ahmedabad, India ... 30
Figure 19 *Source:* https://en.wikipedia.org/w/index.php?title=File:A_Male_Lion_at_Bannargatta_National_Park.jpg *License:* Creative Commons Attribution-Sharealike 3.0 *Contributors:* User:Mydreamsparrow ... 30
Figure 20 *Source:* https://en.wikipedia.org/w/index.php?title=File:Lion_cubs_(4031355883).jpg *Contributors:* Llyfrgell Genedlaethol Cymru / The National Library of Wales from Wales/Cymru ... 32
Figure 21 *Source:* https://en.wikipedia.org/w/index.php?title=File:Guided_tour_with_Lions,_Botlierskop_(South_Africa).jpg *Contributors:* User:Olga Ernst ... 33
Figure 22 *Source:* https://en.wikipedia.org/w/index.php?title=File:Albrecht_Dürer_-_Two_seated_lions_-_Google_Art_Project.jpg *License:* Public Domain *Contributors:* Boo-Boo Baroo, OgreBot 2, Oursana ... 34
Figure 23 *Source:* https://en.wikipedia.org/w/index.php?title=File:Lion_-_melbourne_zoo.jpg *Contributors:* Basvb, BotMultichill, Elekhh, Fir0002, SunOfErat, SuperJew, Winterkind ... 35
Figure 24 *Source:* https//en.wikipedia.org *License:* Creative Commons Attribution-Sharealike 2.0 *Contributors:* Carole Raddato from FRANKFURT, Germany ... 36
Figure 25 *Source:* https://en.wikipedia.org/w/index.php?title=File:Lion_tamer_(LOC_pga.03749).jpg *License:* Public Domain *Contributors:* Gibson & Co., publisher ... 37
Figure 26 *Source:* https://en.wikipedia.org/w/index.php?title=File:Lionsoftsavo2008.jpg *License:* Creative Commons Attribution-Sharealike 3.0,2.5,2.0,1.0 *Contributors:* Superx308 Jeffrey Jung email: superx308 at gmail.com ... 38
Figure 27 *Source:* https://en.wikipedia.org/w/index.php?title=File:Lions_painting,_Chauvet_Cave_(museum_replica).jpg *License:* Public Domain *Contributors:* HTO ... 40

License

Index

www.ingramcontent.com/pod-product-compliance
Lightning Source LLC
Chambersburg PA
CBHW022342280326
41934CB00006B/747